Assertiveness

"How Can I Say What I Mean?"

by Kate Havelin

Consultant:
Marion London, MEd
National Director, Project Charlie
Program of Storefront/Youth Action

Perspectives on Relationships

LifeMatters
an imprint of Capstone Press
Mankato, Minnesota

LifeMatters books are published by Capstone Press
818 North Willow Street • Mankato, Minnesota 56001
http://www.capstone-press.com

Printed in the United States of America

Library of Congress Cataloging-in-Publication Data
Havelin, Kate, 1961–
    Assertiveness: how can I say what I mean? / by Kate Havelin.
        p.   cm. — (Perspectives on relationships)
    Includes bibliographical references and index.
    Summary: Defines assertiveness, discusses its value, and offers strategies for readers to improve their assertiveness skills.
    ISBN 0-7368-0290-8 (book). — ISBN 0-7368-0295-9 (series)
    1. Assertiveness in adolescence. [1. Assertiveness (Psychology)]
    I. Title. II. Series.
    BF724.3.A77H38 2000
    158.2—dc21   99-35386
                                       CIP

Staff Credits
Anita Larsen, Kristin Thoennes, editors; Adam Lazar, designer; Kimberly Danger, photo researcher

Text Credits
Chapter 1: Angela Evans "Why Do Girls Rank Themselves?" *YO!* (October, 1997)

Photo Credits
Cover: The Stock Market/©Jon Feingersh
Photri Inc/©B. Kulik, 9; ©Skjold, 11; ©Photri Inc, 33; ©Robert W. Ginn, 36; ©D&I MacDonald; ©Skjold, 45
PNI/©DigitalVision, 22
Unicorn Stock Photos/©Russell R. Grundke, 15; ©Dennis MacDonald, 22; ©Karen Holsinger Mullen, 25; ©Jeff Greenberg, 26; ©Aneal Vohra, 54
Visuals Unlimited/©Jeff Greenberg, 7; ©Bud Nielsen, 28; ©Jeff Greenberg, 38; ©Deneve Feigh Bunde, 46; ©Jeff Greenberg, 53; ©Mark E. Gibson

Table of Contents

Chapter Overview

Assertive people are confident. They know what they want and work toward their goals in a way that is fair to everyone.

Some people are passive rather than assertive. They may not stand up for their rights. They may let others make decisions for them.

People who are aggressive also know what they want. However, they may hurt others in the process of getting what they want.

Many teens struggle to remain confident. Some young people feel overwhelmed by the number of choices they have. Other teens hurt their self-esteem by comparing themselves negatively with others.

Being assertive can help teens handle changes and challenges.

Chapter 1

What Is Assertiveness?

Karen loves figure skating. **Karen Does Not Compete**
She watched the Olympics
and was amazed to see a skater her own age compete before
the world. Karen cannot imagine how a 14-year-old girl could
handle the pressure. Karen feels comfortable on the ice, but
competing made her tense. Now she skates just for herself. She
does not compete. But Karen wishes she felt as confident as
the kids who do compete seem to feel.

"Far too many people are looking for the right person, instead of trying to be the right person."
—Gloria Steinem

Assertiveness is a big word for a basic idea. People who are assertive stand up for themselves without hurting others. Assertive people have confidence. They can say what they want and think. This book offers tips that can help you become more assertive and confident. After all, anyone can choose to be confident and assertive. It does not cost any money, and it doesn't require any diploma.

Three Styles of Relating to Others

People basically relate to others in one of three ways. They can be assertive, passive, or aggressive. A good method of understanding those three styles of behavior is to imagine three boats.

Assertive

One boat is skimming through the water, heading toward a beautiful island. The captain of that boat knows where she is going. The island is her goal. She is working to achieve her goal without intruding on anyone else. This captain is assertive.

Passive

A second boat is just drifting. The captain of this boat might like to visit the island. But he is not steering his boat. It goes wherever the waves push it. This captain is not in charge of either his boat or his destination. He is passive.

Aggressive

The captain of a third boat wants to get to the island before the other boats. She speeds past the drifting boat, nearly overturning it. Then she cuts in front of the other boat, forcing that boat to change course. This captain arrives at the island first. She achieves her goal by pushing others around and possibly hurting them. She is aggressive.

What Is Behind These Styles?

Assertive people are straightforward. They are clear about their goals and wishes. They stand up for themselves. They are confident. They know how to say what they think. Assertive people usually have strong self-esteem. That means they have a healthy image of themselves and feel good about who they are. It does not mean they think they are perfect, better than others, or always in control.

Assertiveness is one of the key assets that help young people become mature, responsible adults.

In contrast, passive people usually let other people make decisions for them. They may just let things happen. Consequently, they seldom get what they want. People who are passive may not even know what they want to begin with. Then they may be likely to feel disappointed or angry at what they get.

Aggressive people take assertiveness to an unhealthy extreme. They know what they want and stop at little to get it. They are pushy. They often appear to be under pressure and stress. They increase stress for other people, too.

Why Do Teens Need to Be Assertive?

Big changes happen for teens as they become adults. Many young people feel scared and uncertain. They often face serious decisions about school, work, friends, and even sex. Some teens face temptations like alcohol and other drugs. Being assertive makes it easier to make the right decisions for you.

Teens can feel overwhelmed with so many choices. Sometimes it shakes their confidence. For example, deciding whether to aim for college or vo-tech can be frightening. It may be tempting to float and let life just happen to you rather than to set a course.

The Life of the Party

Armand seems like the life of the party. He is always ready for fun. But Armand does not feel confident. He dreads turning 18 and graduating from high school. He does not know what he wants. He feels scared to look ahead. He is frightened to get a job and have to work every day. Armand doesn't study and doubts he could get into college. He hates it when adults ask him what he will do next year. Armand wishes he could stay in high school.

"I graduated from high school this spring, and as I look back on my high school years, I feel sad that I spent so much time criticizing myself and never appreciating who I was."
—Angela Evans

What seems easiest is not always the best choice. Armand may think he is making his life easy now. He hasn't set goals for himself. In that way, he is actually setting himself up for trouble later. People who do not set goals may lose opportunities. Armand may have fewer choices if he makes some decisions after he leaves high school. However, Armand could assertively decide what he wants to do later and still enjoy high school now.

Constant Comparisons Hurt

When teens compare themselves with others, they may lose self-confidence. They think everyone else is better than they are—taller, stronger, funnier, smarter, or more popular. Constantly comparing yourself with others is unhealthy. Assertive people accept themselves as they are. People who accept themselves are happier and healthier than people who compare themselves with others.

Points to Consider

Think of someone you know who seems confident and assertive. How does that person act?

How do you know that a person is assertive?

Close your eyes and imagine yourself answering a question in class. You are prepared. You know your answer is correct. However, you hear another student mutter something and laugh. You look up to see that student and another shaking their heads at each other and looking as if they think you are wrong. Now imagine yourself being assertive. How do you think the rest of the class might treat you?

How do you feel when you compare yourself with others?

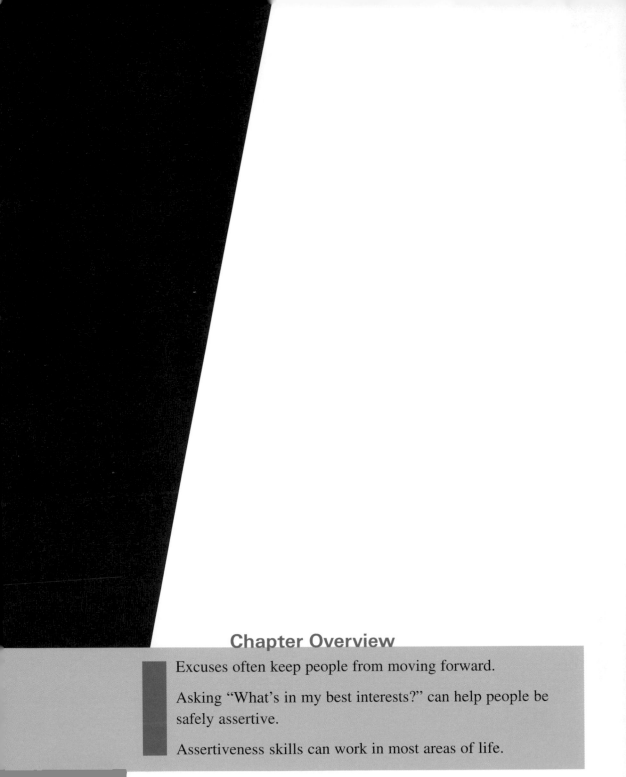

Chapter Overview

Excuses often keep people from moving forward.

Asking "What's in my best interests?" can help people be safely assertive.

Assertiveness skills can work in most areas of life.

Chapter 2

Why Aren't More People Assertive?

Two Friends, Two Points of View

Emmanuel feels shy. He dreams of waking up and being someone bigger, stronger, funnier, and smarter. Until that happens, he keeps to himself. He wishes he felt as confident as his friend Jaime seems to. Jaime always seems to know what he wants.

When Jaime likes a girl, he just asks her out. Emmanuel likes Fabi but cannot imagine dating her. Jaime tells Emmanuel not to sweat it so much. "So what if you ask and Fabi says no?" Jaime asks. "Just give it a try." But Emmanuel feels frozen. He is too scared to try.

Excuses, Excuses

Many people have reasons for why they cannot or won't do things. Fear often traps people and keeps them from trying new things. Fearful people believe things will turn out badly. Assertive people feel that a good outcome is possible. However, most people fall back on excuses to remain inactive every now and then. You may have heard or used some of these excuses:

"I don't have the right clothes."

"I'm not smart enough."

"I'll ask her out when my face clears up."

"I'm not going to raise my hand. Someone might laugh at me."

"People will think I'm weird."

"I'd be afraid to do that."

"I'm not as good as they are."

Some people use shyness as a shield. They are a little like a turtle. They feel protected inside their shell. However, even a turtle has to stick its neck out of its shell to move forward. Shy people have to "stick their neck out" when it is important in order to move forward as well. Usually that requires some assertiveness.

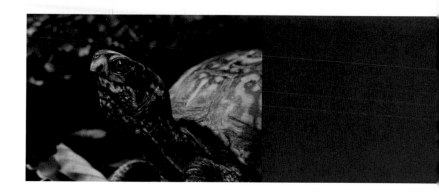

What's in Your Best Interests?

It is not only shy people or turtles who fear "sticking their neck out." Many people avoid putting themselves in the spotlight. Sometimes it is safer not to stand up for yourself assertively. For example, confronting another teen who is carrying a knife may not be the best choice. On the other hand, confronting a person who cuts ahead of you in a ticket line is usually okay. A key question in any situation is "What's in my best interests?"

Chapter 5 describes how to say what you mean assertively in upsetting situations.

Is It Hard to Be Assertive?

It is not hard to learn how to be assertive. Chapters 3 through 6 describe how to build assertiveness skills. Such skills are communicating, setting goals, managing anger, and building self-confidence. Developing these skills may help you relate to others in a healthy way in many areas of your life. The chart on the next page may help you determine how assertive you already may be.

Choose the number in each item below that best describes you.

1 = Never	3 = Sometimes	5 = Always
2 = Rarely	4 = Usually	

1. I do my own thinking and make my own decisions.   1 2 3 4 5
2. I freely express my feelings and beliefs.   1 2 3 4 5
3. I accept responsibility for my life.   1 2 3 4 5
4. I make decisions and accept the consequences.   1 2 3 4 5
5. When I need help, I ask others to help me.   1 2 3 4 5
6. When at fault, I apologize.   1 2 3 4 5
7. When confused, I ask for explanation.   1 2 3 4 5
8. When someone is annoying me, I ask that person to stop.   1 2 3 4 5
9. When treated unfairly, I object.   1 2 3 4 5
10. I ask my doctor all the questions I want answers for.   1 2 3 4 5
11. When I am interrupted, I politely comment on the interruption and then finish what I am saying.   1 2 3 4 5
12. If friends invite me to do something and I really don't want to, I turn down the request.   1 2 3 4 5
13. When someone criticizes me, I listen to the criticism without being defensive.   1 2 3 4 5
14. When one friend is not meeting all my needs, I establish meaningful relationships with many other people.   1 2 3 4 5
15. If I am jealous, I explore the reasons for my feelings. Then I look for other ways to increase my self-confidence.   1 2 3 4 5

Total your score. The higher your score, the greater is your level of assertive behavior. The highest possible score is 75.

You can practice assertiveness skills by speaking to a mirror, or you can try imagining scenes in your mind. Or you can tackle role-playing with others. These three tools are powerful. Using any of them can help you learn how best to do what is in your best interests.

How Assertiveness Can Work

Assertiveness skills can work in many situations. For example, everyone is a member of different communities or groups. You may be a student, a brother or sister, or a daughter or son. You may be an employee, a church member, or a girlfriend or boyfriend. Each role you play takes you into a different group. You can use assertiveness in all these roles or groups.

The following examples explain a little about how or why assertiveness skills can work.

Relating Assertively to the Opposite Sex

Sometimes miscommunication occurs between the genders, or sexes. This may result from a basic difference in male and female styles of relating to others. Some studies show that this difference arises as girls and boys enter adolescence. Many young men may react to the physical changes they experience by becoming aggressive. Many young women may react to the physical changes by becoming passive. Being assertive can be a healthy way to bridge this difference.

This difference may show up on the highway, for example. Juan may want to chase a reckless driver whose car speeds past him and cuts in front of him dangerously close. However, Maria may just want to keep out of the reckless driver's way. An assertive and prudent action might be to report the car's license number.

Relating Assertively to Friends

Being assertive means thinking for yourself and deciding your own actions. Many people think and act exactly as their friends do. However, an assertive person may not do what his or her friends do from time to time. Standing up for yourself at such times may feel uncomfortable. Some people may even worry about what others think. It takes courage and determination to do what is right for you and not fear what others think.

Jamahl Misses Some Good Times

Jamahl is a popular senior, a track star. He has an excellent chance to win the college track scholarship that he has worked so long to achieve.

Jamahl is looking forward to the free time of spring break as much as everyone else. On the other hand, he is not looking forward to the challenges he knows he will face during the break. His friends have already started planning parties. They expect Jamahl to join them. However, breaking training is not in Jamahl's best interests at this time.

Jamahl has practiced what he will say when his friends phone with invitations. He knows the real test will come when he says no to his friends. Jamahl hopes his friends will understand and support his decision not to party. However, he expects that some of his friends will disappoint him. That will sadden him, but it will not stop him.

Points to Consider

Have you ever done something that was not in your best interests? Did you feel as if you were hurting yourself? Why or why not?

How differently do you think the two sexes relate to each other?

Think of a time when you went against the crowd. How did you feel at the time? How did you feel later?

Use the chart to rate your assertiveness. How did you do?

In what ways would you like to become more assertive?

Chapter Overview

Good communication helps people connect.

Healthy communication means that people assertively express what they want or need.

Active listening, supportive responses, and the use of *I* statements are all a part of healthy communication.

Chapter 3

Improve Your Communication

What Is Healthy Communication?

The single best way to let people know what you want is to tell them. It is not safe to assume that others will know what you want or need. Clear communication usually gives people a chance to get what they want. Communication is an important part of being assertive.

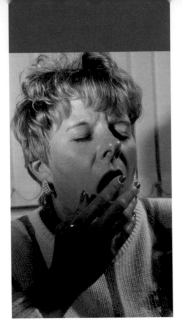

Lauren and Will have been going out **Shall We Dance?** for two months. But lately, the couple has not been getting along. They are not communicating with each other. Lauren thinks Will knows she loves to go dancing. She cannot understand why he keeps taking her to movies instead. Will assumes Lauren likes movies as much as he does. It does not occur to him that Lauren might not want to go to the movies every week.

Movies bore Lauren, but she does not tell Will that. Instead, she makes sneering comments about the movies he selects. Will begins to think Lauren does not like him. Her insults about his flicks, the movies he selects, annoy him. Will does not tell Lauren this for a while. Then one night he explodes. He tells Lauren that if she doesn't like his taste, she can get another boyfriend. A few days later, Lauren tells Will she does not want to go out with him anymore.

True communication happens when two people pay attention to
each other. They try to understand what the other person is feeling.
Good communication helps people connect. Will and Lauren might
have stayed together if they had both said what they wanted.

It is important to realize that talking is not the same as
communicating. Communication includes both speaking and
listening. The following four tactics can help improve your
communication skills.

In some cultures eye contact is not acceptable. Usually in North America, however, it is acceptable.

1. Listen.

Listening is probably the most important part of communication. Yet many people aren't taught this skill. For example, a person may hear the first part of what someone says. Then the person thinks about what to say next rather than hearing the speaker's whole message. Such a listener may interrupt or finish sentences for the speaker. Sometimes the listener looks or acts impatient. This tells the speaker the listener is bored or judging the message.

An active listener concentrates on the other person. An active listener:

Listens carefully to the speaker's words.

Makes eye contact with the speaker.

Observes the speaker's body language.

Thinks about what he or she hears.

Active listening takes effort, but it is a skill worth learning in order to gain true communication.

2. Encourage the speaker.

An active listener encourages the speaker and makes sure he or she understands the message. To do this, the listener paraphrases the speaker's message. Paraphrasing means that the listener puts the message into his or her own words. Here are examples of what an active listener might say:

"If I understand you correctly . . . ."

"It sounds to me like you think that . . . ."

"You sound as if you are feeling . . . ."

Restating the message can draw a speaker out and encourage him or her to say more. So can a clarifying statement like this one:

"When you say _____, do you mean _____?"

The speaker knows the listener is paying attention and trying to understand. Also, the speaker will be more likely to listen closely when it's the listener's turn to talk.

3. Use *I* Statements.

Clear communication also means the speaker clearly expresses his or her thoughts and ideas. A good rule of thumb is to use *I* statements. These statements allow one person to say how he or she feels without putting down the other person.

In the previous story, for example, Lauren could have been honest with Will. Instead, she never clearly stated what she wanted to do. She could have said, "I feel bored at movies. I'd rather go dancing." She ended up resenting sitting in a movie theater instead of moving on a dance floor. Will also could have cleared up his communication with Lauren by telling her how he felt. He could have said, "When you make fun of my flicks, I feel hurt. I would not feel so bad if you would tell me what you'd rather do."

It may take more energy and effort to listen actively, but the results are worth it. With practice, active listening skills will come naturally.

Did You Know?

4. Find a Quiet Place to Talk.

True communication can happen when people pay close attention to each other. Paying attention is easier when the TV, radio, or VCR is switched off. Extra sounds can interfere with a conversation and sometimes confuse it. Let the phone ring if the person speaking really needs a listener. If the call is important, the person will call again. If you cannot find a quiet place to talk, try to make it as quiet as possible.

Some Words to Avoid

Healthy communication means people express what they want or need. It does not help communication to say you don't care what happens. That is being passive. People who are afraid to say what they want may use lines like these:

"Whatever."

"You decide."

"It doesn't matter to me."

These lines are okay if you truly do not care about what happens. However, if you use them when you do care, you will get a outcome different from what you want.

Irina Learns to Say What She Means

Irina wants to make friends in her new school. So she tries to be flexible and let others decide things. Irina goes out for pizza with her new friend, Gwen. Gwen asks Irina what she wants on their pizza. Irina says she likes everything and tells Gwen to order what she wants. While Irina goes to the bathroom, Gwen orders.

When the pizza comes to their table, Irina loses her appetite. She had not expected Gwen to order the "Works" pizza. All Irina can think of is how much all the toppings cost. Since she let Gwen choose them, Irina does not complain. She quietly scrapes some of the toppings off her slices of pizza. Next time, Irina promises herself, she will be clear about what she wants.

Points to Consider

With whom do you communicate well? Why do you think
it is easy to communicate with some people and not with
others?

Do you think it takes more effort to use active listening than
not to? Why?

What do you think it would be like to listen more than you
talk for a day?

Why do you think so many people have trouble
communicating?

Chapter Overview

Setting goals is a way to take control of your life.

Everyone needs goals.

It is possible to set long-term, mid-term, and short-term goals.

Writing goals down and working with one or more other people are two ways to help people achieve their goals.

Chapter 4

Set Goals and Go for Them

Many young people feel they have no control of their lives. They feel parents, teachers, coaches, or friends have more power than they do. However, young people have more power than they might think. Lucinda's story on the next page is an example.

Lucinda's boyfriend **Lucinda Takes Responsibility** Sean said the only gift he wanted for his 16th birthday was Lucinda's picture. Lucinda asked her mom if she could get a really great studio portrait taken. "Good idea," Mom said. "Your 16th birthday is soon, too. I'd like a copy of the picture. Why don't you set it up?" Lucinda rushed to make an appointment.

Lucinda was ready for her appointment, but no one was home to take her. Maybe Mom had forgotten. Dad was out of town on business. Taking a bus would wreck Lucinda's hair, and she did not have cash for cab fare. But she had a learner's permit, and Dad's car was in the garage.

Lucinda's permit allowed her to drive only when an adult was in the car. However, Lucinda took Dad's car. She could not believe it when she got home and Mom grounded her for a week. "I'm sorry, Lucinda, but choices have consequences," Mom said. "I apologize for being late and not phoning you. You must have been on pins and needles. But if you'd had an accident, your dad and I would have been in trouble, too."

"I guess I was not thinking of that, Mom," Lucinda said. "This picture was more important to me than anything else at the time. Nothing bad happened on the drive there and back, and I don't like being grounded. But I can understand where you're coming from. Next time, I'll say when something is really important to me. Can I rely on you to remember it?"

Lucinda's mom smiled. "Yes, you can," she said, nodding. "I promise. No more pins-and-needles stuff from me."

Lucinda could have felt like a victim. However, she accepted responsibility for her actions. She recognized that she had some control from the start. She saw that she could have told her mom up front how important the picture was. She could have phoned to see if her mom was on her way home before she used her dad's car. Heavy traffic or accidents can destroy schedules. She also could have given some thought to alternate transportation to get to her appointment.

However, in the pressure of the moment, Lucinda pushed aside her responsibilities. She ignored the terms of her learner's permit. That meant that she lost privileges like going out with friends for a time.

"You can't make someone else's choices. You shouldn't let someone else make yours."
—U.S. Army General Colin Powell

The important part of Lucinda's story is how she assertively claimed her right to be listened to and respected by her mom. The positive way Lucinda made her claim instantly won her mom's approval. That was exactly the goal Lucinda had in mind. She went for what was important rather than complain about the small stuff. Setting goals can help people get clear about what is important. Knowing what is important can help resolve arguments before they even get started.

Everyone Needs Goals

As a teen, you may be at a turning point. Within the next few years, you will become fully responsible for your life. You may be faced with big decisions like where to live, and whether to work or go to school.

Close your eyes and dream about what you want to look like in 10 years. Do you see yourself wearing a suit and working in a big office? Do you want to own a car, house, or boat? What do you think it would take to reach your goals?

How can you feel ready for those responsibilities? Instead of trying to decide what to do with your whole life, you might start small. For example, you might decide what you want to accomplish this week. A typical teen may want to:

Spend time with friends.

Earn Bs instead of Cs.

Use the family car two nights a week.

Get along better with his or her family.

Get a part-time job and save money.

Buy a car.

Find a date for the prom.

What do *you* want? The list above may trigger your own ideas.

Most people have to be willing to work to get what they want. Think carefully about each item on your list. What will it take to get what you want? Are you willing to do what it takes? For example, are you willing to spend extra time studying to earn better grades? Are you willing to work extra hours to save money?

Set Realistic Goals

It can be tough to turn a life around in a flash. It takes time to break habits. For example, a D student may truly want better grades. However, it may not be realistic to expect straight As on the next report card. That student can decide, however, to pull all her grades up to at least C. In another area of your life, maybe you and your parents don't get along. Repairing a relationship takes time and effort.

It is a good idea to set long-term, mid-term, and short-term goals. You can work on several goals at the same time. For example, you can go for a run today. At the same time, you are working on being physically fit 10 years from now.

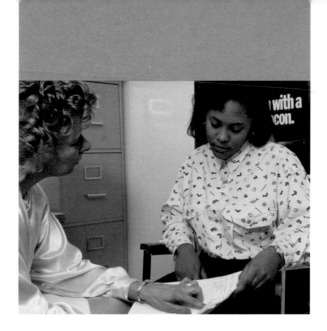

Mai Works on Her Goals

Mai has thought about what she wants her life to be. She wants to go to college. She wants to have a good job and a nice apartment. Achieving those goals seems distant. But right now Mai is doing what she can to make those far-off goals come true.

She has talked with her school guidance counselor about how to get financial aid for college. The counselor said Mai should work on improving her grades. She also suggested Mai get a summer job to gain work experience and build savings.

Here are some of Mai's goals:

Short-term goal: Study every night.

Mid-term goal: Save $2 a week from allowance.

Long-term goal: Apply to eight places during spring break for a summer job.

Techniques to Help Meet Your Goals

It can be hard to reach a goal. These two techniques may keep you moving forward.

1. Write down your goals.

It helps to put a goal in writing. Seeing a goal on paper can make it more real. Writing down goals also can help make them more doable. Beneath your big goals, you can list minigoals that are steps along the way. Each time you reach a minigoal, check it off. Those checkmarks will give you a feeling of accomplishment.

2. Share a goal with a friend.

It helps to work toward a goal with someone else. Another person can help keep you motivated. All kinds of goals are more easily achieved in company with others. For example, many people exercise more often if they do it with friends. Some people study better with others. Or maybe you and a friend could walk to the library, study, and then get a snack afterward. You'd study, get exercise, and reward yourself.

"Setting goals and writing them down is one of the most important things you can do. Commit them to memory, stay focused, and develop the stamina to go the distance. If you do, you can achieve any goal you set."
—Tara Lipinsky, Olympic gold medal skater

Points to Consider

Think about a goal that is important to you. What are you doing to reach that goal?

What else could you do to work toward your goals?

Write down three personal goals. Make one a short-term goal, one a mid-term goal, and one a long-term goal.

Choose one goal to share with a friend. Why do you think it might help to have another person working toward the same goal?

Chapter Overview

People can decide how to respond when they are upset. A "time out" can lead to a calmer way to communicate.

To handle tough problems, identify what bothers you, describe how you feel, and then think of a solution.

People cannot control how other people act or react.

Chapter 5

Manage Your Anger

Kieran is furious. His younger brother, Ian, borrowed his favorite shirt without asking. Then Ian spilled spaghetti sauce on it.

Before, Kieran would have yelled at Ian. The two would end up hitting each other until their parents stepped in. Now Kieran has learned better ways to settle problems. He knows he should cool down. He takes a "time out." Five minutes later, he can think clearly about the situation. When he feels he can stay in control, he approaches Ian.

"Ian," Kieran says, "I found my shirt in the dirty laundry. It is stained. I can't wear it tonight to the concert. That was my favorite shirt, and I really wanted to wear it. I'm mad that I can't wear it. I want you to ask me before you go into my room or borrow my things."

What to Say When Someone Upsets You

Most people feel angry from time to time. Even good friends can upset you. If anger is not managed well, it can turn into aggression. Assertive people know how to channel their anger. An assertive person can identify the problem, describe his or her feelings, and suggest a solution.

Identify the problem.

People can feel angry because of what someone else did. The other person may not realize his or her actions were upsetting or that anything is wrong. It is important to explain simply and clearly what angered you.

It does not help to be aggressive and attack the other person with accusations or name-calling. Doing so may only anger the other person. More fighting will not solve the problem. A good method is to focus on the action that upset you rather than the person who did it. Here's an example of Keiran's before-and-after words to his brother:

Before	After
"You're a jerk. I can't believe you wrecked my favorite shirt."	"My shirt is stained, and now I can't wear it."

The fight-or-flight reaction started in prehistoric times when humans faced deadly threats like saber-toothed tigers. Prehistoric humans had to decide whether to fight a tiger or flee from it. Now few people face tigers, but they still feel the same fight-or-flight reaction to tense situations.

Describe how you feel.

It's important to know that there are some steps you can take to manage your anger. These steps are:

Stay calm.

Stick to how you feel.

Focus your anger on the *problem*, not the *person*.

Use *I* statements.

I statements help you describe how you feel, not what you think of the other person. When upset, your thoughts may be negative judgments. People may feel like they must defend themselves from your judgmental comments. More anger simply sparks more tension. It does not resolve the problem.

At times, the most powerful apology you can make is a heartfelt "I'm sorry."

Here are examples of how to turn judgmental statements into assertive, nonjudgmental statements:

Before	After
"How dare you yell at me? Don't ever yell at me again!"	"I don't like being yelled at. I feel angry when you yell at me."
"I heard what you said about me, you two-faced liar. You are no friend of mine."	"I don't understand why you said those mean things about me. I feel sad and confused."

Think of a solution.

Almost every problem has a solution. The solution may not be perfect, but it can make a bad situation better. Here are some problem-solving steps:

Identify what the problem is.

Think clearly to see what causes the problem.

List as many options to solve the problem as you can think of.

Consider the consequences of each option.

If the problem is between friends, negotiate, or talk together, about what can settle the problem.

Decide on an option you think will solve the problem.

Carry out the solution.

Evaluate the outcome.

Try again if the first solution doesn't work.

Shannon feels crushed. The girl she considered her best friend, Cassie, has gossiped about her. Shannon told Cassie the cruel rumors hurt her feelings. She asked Cassie to tell people they weren't true. Cassie just laughed.

Sometimes Life Is Not Fair

Shannon knows Cassie is lying. But she does not know how to convince her other friends of that. Shannon talks to her mom, who reminds her that true friends will stick by her. Shannon decides she will continue to be a good friend to people she likes. She figures the best way to have a good friend is to be one. But she wishes she could be certain of what others think of her.

You Cannot Control Other People

It is important to realize that people cannot control other people. No matter how reasonable or pleasant you are, others may be unreasonable in return. No matter how reasonable your solution to a problem, others may refuse to accept it.

It is also important to know that the only person you can control is you. You can decide how you want to act and react. You can choose to get more or less upset by how other people act.

Points to Consider

How do you react when you are upset? Do you take time to cool down before talking to the person who upset you?

Think of a time when you blew up at someone. How could you have handled that situation better?

Why do you think it is important not to put others on the defensive?

How do you react when someone says something judgmental to you?

Chapter Overview

People can choose to believe in themselves.

Everyone is good at something.

Accepting mistakes can help control the fear of doing new things.

People can boost their confidence by making decisions for themselves.

Choose friends who make you feel good about yourself.

Chapter 6

Ways to Build Self-Confidence

Stella Imagines the Worst

Stella feels confident in the classroom. However, she is nervous around girls she likes. For example, Stella can see herself dropping her books in front of Lara. She imagines Lara laughing at her and joking about her clumsiness. When Stella sees Lara in the hall, she blushes. She clutches her books to her chest and hurries by without saying hi.

Stretching Your Comfort Zone

Some people wait their whole life to feel relaxed and confident. You may feel confident at some times and not at others. It is easier to be assertive when you feel relaxed. Here are several ways to stretch your comfort zone and perhaps feel more confident.

"You just gotta believe. You've got to believe in yourself. If you don't believe in yourself, nobody else will."
—Deion Sanders

Choose to believe in yourself.

People have the power to shape their life through the choices they make. One of those choices is how they see themselves. They can choose to imagine themselves as positive and successful. On the other hand, they can decide to see themselves as hopeless. Chances are, the way they imagine themselves is the way they will be.

Most people like to feel good about themselves. It is within their power to create a positive image for themselves. For example, in the previous story Stella let negative pictures run in her head. She could try replacing those bad images with more positive ones. She could imagine herself talking easily with Lara as she helped pick up the books. How you imagine connecting with people can shape real-life encounters.

At a
Glance

To learn what kind of image you have of yourself, listen to yourself. Almost everyone has mental tapes. Our tapes are what we say to ourselves. What do your tapes sound like? They should be as generous to yourself as you are to your friends.

What you tell yourself also can change outcomes. For example, what do you think before a big test? Some teens use positive self-talk such as, "I can do it. I've gone to class and done the homework. I know I can do my best on this test." Others use negative self-talk such as "I'm going to flunk. I am just not good in math. I don't care how I do."

People who use positive self-talk often do better than those who use negative self-talk. Thoughts can be powerful.

Focus on skills you already have.
Everyone is good at something. For example, some people are great cooks. Others can walk or run for miles without wearing out. Maybe you are a good listener. That skill can help you all your life. Thinking of your strengths is a way to build a positive image of yourself.

"Don't let fear of failure hold you back. It is not a tragedy to strive for something and not achieve it. It is a tragedy to never try."
—Rosalynn Carter

Another way to build a positive self-image is to think about what you like to do. For instance, you may have a hobby you like so much that you spend hours at it. Just thinking about your hobby makes you feel confident and powerful. The strong feeling you have doing something you like can help build your confidence.

Accept mistakes.
People's imaginary fears often keep them from trying things they want to do. For example, Stella's fears that she might drop her books made her avoid Lara. A healthier attitude is to accept that mistakes will happen. So what if Stella dropped her books? Lara might have helped her pick them up.

Accepting mistakes is a powerful way to control fears. Everyone makes mistakes occasionally—even assertive people. However, assertive people do not stop trying because they fear making a mistake. When people are assertive, they show respect for themselves by accepting their mistakes. That attitude may gain respect from others.

Make your own decisions.

Assertive people make decisions for themselves without harming the rights of others. Making your own decisions requires that you trust your judgment. Each decision you make boosts your self-confidence. The decisions do not have to be major choices. For example, you can shop for a shirt by yourself. Or you can choose to eat salad for lunch when all your friends are eating pizza.

Choose the right friends.

Most people value friendship. However, some people choose friends for reasons other than to have a close relationship. Such people might value a friend for his or her car more than for himself or herself. Or they like the idea of who their friend knows more than they like their friend. A friendship based solely on considerations like these seldom builds self-confidence.

On the other hand, choosing friends who make you feel good about yourself does build self-confidence. Talking about a good experience with someone who shared it can make what happened even better. Supporting a friend's accomplishment makes you part of a winning team. It is more fun to laugh with someone who is laughing along with you. True friends make it easy to feel relaxed and confident.

Dylan got into a lot of trouble at his old school. This year, his parents

Dylan Reaches Out

switched Dylan to a new school, and he decided to start fresh. He made the effort to talk with kids he did not know. He asked different people if he could eat lunch with them. Soon some boys invited Dylan to play basketball with them.

Sometimes Dylan is lonely. But now when he starts to imagine that he will never fit in, he stops himself immediately. He changes his mental tape and thinks ahead to when he will have lots of real friends. Dylan feels confident that those positive images will soon become reality.

Points to Consider

Who do you believe has the power to shape your life?

Do you think others treat people who are positive and people who are negative differently? Why or why not?

Think of something you like to do and how you feel when you do that. What can you do to feel that way all the time?

Close your eyes and imagine the best way your life could be. How does that make you feel? How do you feel when you think about the worst possible happenings? Why do you think imagining positive things makes a difference?

Chapter Overview

People have the power to shape their life.

Goals give direction and purpose to life.

Communication connects people

Assertive people are kind to themselves.

Chapter 7

Important Stuff to Remember

Assertiveness is within your reach. You can decide to become more confident. You can choose to boost your self-esteem. The following points are worth remembering:

1. People have the power to shape their life.
The key to being assertive is to believe in yourself. You can choose to have faith in your abilities. Healthy self-esteem can ease life's challenges.

2. Goals give direction and purpose.
It is difficult to map out a whole life. However, you can choose a direction to head in. Setting goals can give you a clear sense of purpose. Set up short-term goals you can achieve quickly. Do what you can now toward achieving long-term goals.

3. Communication connects people.

Knowing how to communicate can help you connect with people. It takes effort to listen actively. That effort is amply repaid. Learning how to talk, listen, and stay calm when angry are valuable skills. Communication skills become second nature with practice.

4. Assertive people are kind to themselves.

Assertive people treat themselves as well as they treat their friends. Accept that you will make mistakes from time to time. Do what you can to learn from mistakes, but do not dwell on them.

Let your imagination show you success. Then do what you can to make that success happen. Replace negative worries with positive mental tapes.

Avoid constantly comparing yourself with others. Anyone can find someone who is smarter, taller, richer, funnier, or braver than they are. So what? You can be the best you can be.

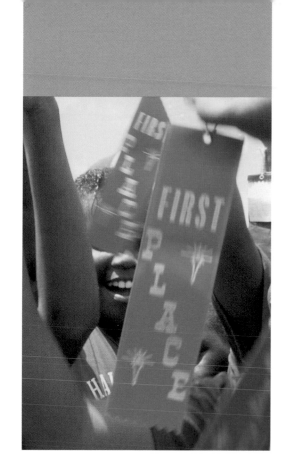

Points to Consider

List three ways you are kind to yourself. How can you use this list when you are presented with new challenges?

How do you feel when you accept mistakes you've made? Does that feeling make a difference in how you approach the next thing you do?

Write a motto for yourself. This can be one word you repeat privately throughout the day like "Winner!" Or it can be a short phrase like "I can do it!"

Glossary

aggressive (uh-GRESS-iv)—pushy, fierce, or threatening; aggressive people bully people out of fear, not confidence.

anger (ANG-gur)—a powerful feeling of being annoyed or upset; assertive people learn to manage their anger instead of having the anger manage them.

assertive (uh-SUR-tiv)—able to stand up for yourself

clarify (KLA-ruh-fye)—to make something clear

confident (KON-fuh-duhnt)—having a strong belief in your own abilities

focus (FOH-kuhss)—to concentrate your attention or energy on something or someone; focusing on your goals can help you achieve them.

gender (JEN-dur)—the sex of a person or creature

goal (GOHL)—a purpose or target you try to reach

judgmental (JUHJ-mehn-tuhl)—involving negative opinions about things or people; judgmental statements often convey blame, anger, or outrage.

negotiate (ni-GOH-shee-ate)—to bargain or discuss something so that you can come to an agreement

paraphrase (PA-ruh-fraze)—to say or write something in a different way

passive (PASS-iv)—describing a person who does not take control

self-esteem (SELF ess-TEEM)—having pride and respect for yourself and your abilities

For More Information

CityKids. *CityKids Speak On Relationships.* New York: Random House, 1994.

Covey, Sean. *The 7 Habits of Highly Effective Teens: The Ultimate Teenage Success Guide.* New York: Simon & Schuster, 1998.

Folkers, Gladys, and Jeanne Engelmann. *Taking Charge of My Mind and Body: A Girls' Guide to Outsmarting Alcohol, Drugs, Smoking, and Eating Problems.* Minneapolis: Free Spirit, 1997.

Ignoffo, Matthew. *Everything You Need to Know About Self-Confidence.* New York: Rosen, 1996.

Useful Addresses and Internet Sites

The CityKids Foundation
57 Leonard Street
New York, NY 10013
www.citykids.com

National Health Services, Knowledge
Exchange Network
PO Box 42490
Washington, DC 20015
1-800-789-2647
www.mentalhealth.org

National Self-Help Clearinghouse
City University of New York
25 West 43rd Street, Room 620
New York, NY 10036
www.selfhelpweb.org

The Self-Help Resource Centre of Greater
Toronto
40 Orchard View Boulevard, Suite 219
Toronto, ON M4R 1B9
CANADA

Girl Power!
www.health.org/gpower
A U.S. Department of Health and Human
Services campaign to increase self-confidence
in girls aged 9 to 14

The National Association for Self-Esteem
www.self-esteem-nase.org
Promotes self-esteem through a research
center, educational programs, and other efforts

Teen Voices
www.teenvoices.com
A quarterly on-line and print magazine by
nonprofit Women Express, Inc.

YO! Youth Outlook
www.pacificnews.org/yo
A monthly on-line and print publication by
Pacific News Service

Index

Index continued